juices & smoothies

The NINJA Kitchen System FLIP Cookbook

Pascoe Publishing, Inc.

Rocklin, CA

Although every precaution has been taken in the preparation of this book, the publisher and authors assume no responsibility for errors or omissions. Nor is any liability assumed for damages resulting from the use of the information contained herein. Although every effort has been made to ensure that the information contained in this book is complete and accurate, neither the publisher nor the authors are engaged in rendering professional advice or services to the individual reader. This information is not intended to replace the advice of a medical practitioner and consumers should always consult with a health care professional prior to making changes to diet or lifestyle, including any new health-related eating programs. Neither the publisher nor author shall be held responsible for any loss or damage allegedly arising from any information or suggestion in this book. The opinions expressed in this book represent the personal views of the authors and not that of the publisher.

Nutritional Analyses: Calculations for the nutritional analyses in this book are based on the largest number of servings listed within the recipes. Calculations are rounded up to the nearest gram or milligram, as appropriate. If two options for an ingredient are listed, the first one is used. Not included are optional ingredients or serving suggestions.

Design: KB Designs • Photography: Austin Blanco • Additional Photography: Shutterstock

Published in the United States of America by

Pascoe Publishing, Inc.
Rocklin, California
www.pascoepublishing.com

ISBN: 978-1-929862-49-8

10   9   8   7   6   5

Printed in China

introduction

We are so sure you are going to FLIP for your new Ninja™ Kitchen System, we've created this FLIP cookbook, *Juices & Smoothies ~ Soups, Sides, Entrées & More!*, to go with it! One half of these delicious recipes are dedicated to frozen, blended drinks, juices and smoothies you'll love and the other half are for quick prep and easy serving of soups, salads, sauces, entrées and desserts. All you have to do is flip the book to discover new tasty sensations and mouth-watering favorites!

Using the pitcher, large-capacity bowl, or single serving cups, you now have the choice of making one cup of fresh juice or enough for the whole family. You can chop and mix in the large-capacity bowl to prep all your meals, and you can use the dough blade to make family-friendly desserts and whole-grain breads. With so many delicious recipes and the Ninja™ Kitchen System ready to do the work for you, we invite you to get started today!

To Your Good Health,

The Ninja™ Team

strawberry banana smoothie

SERVES 1

½ cup apple juice

½ cup low fat plain yogurt

¾ cup fresh strawberries, stemmed and hulled

½ banana, peeled

5 to 6 ice cubes

Place all ingredients in the Single Serve Cup. Pulse until smooth. Serve right away.

CALORIES 224

FAT 2G

CHOL 7MG

SODIUM 19MG

CARB 45G

FIBER 4G

PROTEIN 8G

Juices & Smoothies

blueberry blast

SERVES 1

½ cup white grape juice

½ cup low fat plain yogurt

½ banana, peeled

½ cup fresh or frozen wild blueberries, rinsed

8 ice cubes

Place all ingredients in the Single Serve Cup and pulse until smooth.

CALORIES 252

FAT 2G

CHOL 7MG

SODIUM 97MG

CARB 54G

FIBER 4G

PROTEIN 8G

pomegranate power smoothie

SERVES 1

½ cup low fat plain yogurt

½ cup pomegranate juice

½ cup frozen blueberries

1 tbsp. raw, unfiltered honey

Place all ingredients in the Single Serve Cup and pulse until smooth.

CALORIES 223

FAT 2G

CHOL 7MG

SODIUM 118MG

CARB 50G

FIBER 2G

PROTEIN 7G

6

Juices & Smoothies

sweet cherry smoothie

SERVES 1

½ cup low fat milk

½ cup low fat vanilla yogurt

½ cup fresh sweet cherries, pitted (or use frozen
cherries, if desired)

½ banana, peeled

5 to 6 ice cubes

Place all ingredients in the Single Serve Cup and pulse
until smooth.

CALORIES 239

FAT 2G

CHOL 10MG

SODIUM 134MG

CARB 46G

FIBER 12G

PROTEIN 10G

kale & date smoothie

SERVES 1

¾ cup fresh orange juice

½ cup nonfat vanilla yogurt

½ banana, peeled

½ cup fresh kale, tightly packed

1 date, pitted

5 to 6 ice cubes

Place all ingredients in the Single Serve Cup. Pulse until smooth. Serve right away.

CALORIES 363

FAT 0G

CHOL 3MG

SODIUM 101MG

CARB 87G

FIBER 6G

PROTEIN 9G

summer berry sensation

SERVES 1

½ cup apple juice

½ cup low fat vanilla frozen yogurt

¼ cup frozen raspberries

¼ cup frozen blueberries

¼ cup frozen strawberries

Place all ingredients in the Single Serve Cup and pulse until smooth. Serve right away.

CALORIES 266

FAT 3G

CHOL 10MG

SODIUM 66MG

CARB 55G

FIBER 5G

PROTEIN 11G

green pear smoothie

SERVES 1

½ cup baby spinach leaves
½ ripe Bartlett pear, peeled and cored
½ banana, peeled
5 to 6 ice cubes

Place all ingredients in the Single Serve Cup and pulse until smooth. Strain before serving, if desired. Serve right away.

pineapple papaya smoothie

SERVES 1

¼ cup papaya juice

½ cup fresh pineapple, cut into chunks

½ cup fresh papaya

½ cup low fat vanilla yogurt

5 to 6 ice cubes

Place all ingredients in the Single Serve Cup and pulse until smooth.

CALORIES 191

FAT 1G

CHOL 5MG

SODIUM 79MG

CARB 41G

FIBER 2G

PROTEIN 5G

quick orangesicle

SERVES 1

1 cup low fat vanilla frozen yogurt

¼ cup orange juice

½ cup fresh orange, peeled, segmented

Place all ingredients in the Single Serve Cup and pulse until smooth. Serve right away.

CALORIES 287

FAT 0G

CHOL 4MG

SODIUM 122MG

CARB 64G

FIBER 3G

PROTEIN 1G

Juices & Smoothies

pumpkin ginger smoothie

SERVES 1

½ cup pumpkin puree

½ cup orange juice

½ cup low fat vanilla yogurt

⅛ tsp. fresh ginger

pinch ground cinnamon (optional)

raw, unfiltered honey (optional)

5 to 6 ice cubes

Place all ingredients in the Single Serve Cup and pulse until smooth.

CALORIES 364

FAT 0G

CHOL 4MG

SODIUM 403MG

CARB 84G

FIBER 11G

PROTEIN 3G

almond & dark molasses dream

SERVES 1

¼ cup almond milk

1 tsp. blackstrap molasses

1 cup low fat vanilla frozen yogurt

¼ tsp. pure almond extract (optional)

Place all ingredients in the Single Serve Cup and pulse until smooth.

CALORIES 288

FAT 7G

CHOL 30MG

SODIUM 179MG

CARB 58G

FIBER 0G

PROTEIN 6G

mocha freeze

SERVES 1

½ cup strong coffee, cooled

½ cup low fat chocolate frozen yogurt

1 oz. dark chocolate

5 to 6 ice cubes

Place all ingredients in the Single Serve Cup and pulse until smooth. Serve right away.

CALORIES 318

FAT 13G

CHOL 17MG

SODIUM 85MG

CARB 47G

FIBER 5G

PROTEIN 7G

emerald green elixir

SERVES 1

½ cup white grape juice

½ small banana, peeled

½ cup baby spinach leaves

1 kiwi, peeled

2 tsp. raw, unfiltered honey

5 to 6 ice cubes

Place all ingredients in the Single Serve Cup and pulse until smooth. Serve right away.

CALORIES 220

FAT 0G

CHOL 0MG

SODIUM 25MG

CARB 51G

FIBER 4G

PROTEIN 2G

Juices & Smoothies

mango lassi

SERVES 1

½ cup mango chunks, frozen
½ cup low fat plain yogurt
¼ cup mango juice or milk
1 tsp. raw, unfiltered honey
pinch ground cardamom

Place all ingredients in the Single Serve Cup and pulse until smooth.

CALORIES 225

FAT 2G

CHOL 7MG

SODIUM 92MG

CARB 47G

FIBER 2G

PROTEIN 6G

avocado shake

SERVES 1

½ ripe avocado, pitted and peeled
½ cup low fat milk
1 tbsp. raw, unfiltered honey
8 ice cubes

Place all ingredients in the Single Serve Cup and pulse until smooth. Serve at once.

dandy green machine

SERVES 1

½ cup apple juice

½ cup Swiss chard, rinsed, roughly torn

½ banana, peeled

2 tbsp. goji berries

6 to 8 ice cubes

Place the ingredients in the Single Serve Cup and pulse until smooth. Serve right away.

CALORIES 220

FAT 1G

CHOL 0MG

SODIUM 115MG

CARB 54G

FIBER 6G

PROTEIN 5G

gala apple celebration

SERVES 1

½ cup apple juice

½ ripe Gala apple, cored, roughly cut

½ cup collard greens, rinsed, ribs removed

½ cup nonfat plain yogurt

pinch ground cardamom

5 to 6 ice cubes

Place all ingredients in the Single Serve Cup and pulse until smooth. Strain before serving, if desired.

CALORIES 211

FAT 0G

CHOL 0MG

SODIUM 97MG

CARB 47G

FIBER 4G

PROTEIN 7G

Juices & Smoothies

carrot protein power

SERVES 1

½ cup apple juice

½ small carrot, roughly cut

¼ small ripe Granny Smith apple

½ banana, peeled

1 tbsp. whey protein powder

5 to 6 ice cubes

Place all ingredients in the Single Serve Cup and pulse until smooth. Strain before serving, if desired.

CALORIES 271

FAT 2G

CHOL 60MG

SODIUM 93MG

CARB 46G

FIBER 5G

PROTEIN 19G

vitamin c cucumber blast

SERVES 1

1 grapefruit, peeled and quartered

1 orange, peeled and quartered

¼ cucumber, peeled

2 to 3 ice cubes

Place all ingredients in the Single Serve Cup. Pulse until smooth.

CALORIES 150

FAT 0G

CHOL 0MG

SODIUM 1MG

CARB 38G

FIBER 6G

PROTEIN 3G

Juices & Smoothies

detox antioxidant juice

SERVES 1

1 apple, cored and quartered

½ stalk celery, quartered

1 cup green tea, cooled

½ lemon, juiced

2 to 3 ice cubes

Place the ingredients in the Single Serve Cup. Pulse until smooth.

CALORIES 109

FAT 0G

CHOL 0MG

SODIUM 6MG

CARB 28G

FIBER 4G

PROTEIN 3G

rainbow juice

SERVES 1

4 large strawberries, stemmed

¼ cup pineapple, roughly cut

½ cup greens (use spinach, collard greens,
      dandelion greens or kale)

⅓ cup water

2 to 3 ice cubes

Place all ingredients in the Single Serve Cup. Pulse until smooth.

CALORIES 53

FAT 0G

CHOL 0MG

SODIUM 14MG

CARB 12G

FIBER 3G

PROTEIN 1G

Juices & Smoothies

veggie fusion

SERVES 1

⅛ cucumber, cut into 2 wedges,
    3 inches in length

2 baby carrots

1 small stalk celery, cut in half to
    3 inches in length

½ cup spinach leaves, lightly packed

¼ ripe tomato

7 red or green seedless grapes

¼ to ⅓ cup watermelon, cut into chunks

3 to 4 orange slices, peeled

2 fresh strawberries (or use frozen)

2 to 4 ice cubes

Place all the ingredients in the Single Serve Cup. Pulse until smooth.

CALORIES 42

FAT 0G

CHOL 0MG

SODIUM 32MG

CARB 19G

FIBER 2G

PROTEIN 1G

fresh citrus squeeze

SERVES 1

¼ cup fresh orange juice

½ cup fresh red grapefruit, peeled, segmented

½ cup fresh orange, peeled, segmented

½ cup low fat plain yogurt

1 tsp. powdered sugar

6 ice cubes

Place all ingredients in the Single Serve Cup and pulse until smooth. Serve right away.

carrot apple refresher

SERVES 1

½ cup carrot juice

½ small carrot, peeled, roughly cut

½ small ripe Granny Smith apple, peeled,
    roughly cut

¼ cup low fat plain yogurt

1 tsp. raw, unfiltered honey (or to taste)

pinch ground cloves

5 to 6 ice cubes

Place all ingredients in the Single Serve Cup and pulse until smooth.

CALORIES 183

FAT 0G

CHOL 2MG

SODIUM 93MG

CARB 26G

FIBER 3G

PROTEIN 1G

Juices & Smoothies

garden veggies in a glass

SERVES 1

½ cup apple juice

½ small ripe tomato, peeled, cut in half

½ inner stalk celery, with leaves

1 tbsp. fresh flat-leaf parsley

½ green onion, roughly cut

pinch salt

¼ tsp. ground black pepper

Place all ingredients in the Single Serve Cup and pulse until smooth. Strain before serving, if desired.

CALORIES 78

FAT 0G

CHOL 0MG

SODIUM 165MG

CARB 16G

FIBER 2G

PROTEIN 1G

Juices & Smoothies

red grape squeeze

SERVES 1

1 cup frozen, seedless red grapes
½ cup white grape juice
½ cup low fat vanilla yogurt

Place all ingredients in the Single Serve Cup and pulse until smooth.

CALORIES 192

FAT 0G

CHOL 2MG

SODIUM 28MG

CARB 29G

FIBER 0G

PROTEIN 0G

Juices & Smoothies

green tea freeze

SERVES 1

½ cup green tea, cooled
1 cup low fat vanilla frozen yogurt
pinch ground nutmeg
pinch ground cardamom
5 to 6 ice cubes

Place all ingredients in the Single Serve Cup and pulse until smooth.

watermelon & lime smoothie

SERVES 1

¼ cup white grape juice

1 cup seedless watermelon chunks, frozen

½ tsp. lime zest (optional)

1 tsp. raw, unfiltered honey (optional)

Place all ingredients in the Single Serve Cup and pulse until smooth. Serve right away.

CALORIES 141

FAT 0G

CHOL 0MG

SODIUM 7MG

CARB 37G

FIBER 0G

PROTEIN 1G

complete wake-up-call juice

SERVES 1

1 large leaf Swiss chard

½ ripe pear, cored

3 mint leaves

½ cup water

2 to 3 ice cubes

Place all ingredients in the Single Serve Cup. Pulse until smooth.

CALORIES 57

FAT 0G

CHOL 0MG

SODIUM 103MG

CARB 15G

FIBER 4G

PROTEIN 1G

complete super iron juice

SERVES 1

2 to 3 ice cubes

¼ cucumber, peeled

¼ stalk celery, cut in half

½ tart green apple, cored

¼ cup packed   leaves

½ cup water

Place the ingredients in the order listed into the Single Serve Cup. Pack down slightly, if needed. Blend until smooth.

CALORIES 55

FAT 0G

CHOL 0MG

SODIUM 11MG

CARB 13G

FIBER 2G

PROTEIN 0G

complete afterburner juice

SERVES 1

1 cup green grapes

2 medium leaves Romaine lettuce

¼ cucumber, peeled

½ cup water

3 to 4 ice cubes

Place all ingredients in the Single Serve Cup and blend until smooth.

CALORIES 110

FAT 0G

CHOL 0MG

SODIUM 5MG

CARB 28G

FIBER 1G

PROTEIN 1G

34

complete tomato kickstarter juice

SERVES 1

1 cup sweet grape tomatoes

½ thin slice white onion (or more, if desired)

¼ cucumber, peeled

¼ tsp. balsamic vinegar (or more, to taste)

½ cup water

2 to 3 ice cubes

Place all ingredients in the Single Serve Cup. Blend until smooth.

CALORIES 37

FAT 0G

CHOL 0MG

SODIUM 32MG

CARB 7G

FIBER 2G

PROTEIN 1G

complete wild tropics juice

SERVES 1

1 cup fresh pineapple, in chunks

¼ fresh mango, peeled

2 small leaves kale

1 sprig parsley

½ cup water

2 to 3 ice cubes

Place all ingredients in the Single Serve Cup and pulse until smooth.

CALORIES 124

FAT 0G

CHOL 0MG

SODIUM 11MG

CARB 32G

FIBER 3G

PROTEIN 2G

Juices & Smoothies

complete sunny energy juice

SERVES 2

1 orange, peeled and sectioned

1 tangerine, peeled and sectioned

2 tbsp. lemon juice

2 tbsp. apple cider vinegar

2 tbsp. agave (optional)

6 to 8 ice cubes

Place all ingredients in the Single Serve Cup. Pulse until smooth. Serve right away

CALORIES 60

FAT 0G

CHOL 0MG

SODIUM 5MG

CARB 15G

FIBER 3G

PROTEIN 4G

complete garden blend juice

SERVES 1 TO 2

1 ripe tomato, cored and quartered

¼ cup spinach leaves, packed

1 inside celery stalk, with leaves, cut in half

1 2-inch piece red pepper

1 thin slice white onion

2 to 3 ice cubes

Salt and pepper to taste

Place all ingredients in the Single Serve Cup. Press the Single Serve button and pulse until smooth. Serve immediately.

CALORIES 17

FAT 0G

CHOL 0MG

SODIUM 20MG

CARB 4G

FIBER 2G

PROTEIN 1G

Juices & Smoothies

mango melon mint fusion

SERVES 2

½ cup honeydew melon, cut in chunks

½ cup mango, cut in chunks

½ cup cantaloupe, cut in chunks

3 mint leaves

½ cup water

3 to 4 ice cubes

Place all ingredients in the Pitcher and blend until smooth. Serve immediately.

CALORIES 47

FAT 0G

CHOL 0MG

SODIUM 18MG

CARB 10G

FIBER 2G

PROTEIN 2G

apple ginger gladiator

SERVES 1

1 apple, cored, cut in quarters

1 tsp. fresh ginger

1 oz. wheat grass juice

½ cup water

2 to 3 ice cubes

Place the apple, ginger and wheat grass in the Single Serve Cup. Blend until smooth. Add the water and ice cubes and pulse until smooth. Serve right away.

citrus spirulina blast

SERVES 2 TO 3

1 grapefruit, peeled and quartered

1 orange, peeled and quartered

1 cup fresh or frozen pineapple, cut in chunks

2 tbsp. lime juice

1 tsp. spirulina

1 cup water

6 to 8 ice cubes

Place all ingredients in the Pitcher and blend until smooth. Serve right away.

CALORIES 84

FAT 0G

CHOL 0MG

SODIUM 1MG

CARB 21G

FIBER 3G

PROTEIN 1G

green on green

SERVES 1

1 kiwi, peeled and halved

2 small leaves kale

½ Granny Smith apple, cored

½ cup coconut water

2 to 3 ice cubes

Place all ingredients in the Single Serve Cup. Blend until smooth. Serve at once.

CALORIES 123

FAT 0G

CHOL 0MG

SODIUM 134MG

CARB 30G

FIBER 5G

PROTEIN 3G

Juices & Smoothies

watermelon limeade

SERVES 2

2 cups fresh seeded watermelon, rind removed

¼ cup water

4 tbsp. lime juice

2 tbsp. agave

1 tbsp. fresh mint leaves

4-6 ice cubes

Place all ingredients in the Pitcher and blend until smooth. Serve right away.

CALORIES 46

FAT 0G

CHOL 0MG

SODIUM 2MG

CARB 12G

FIBER 1G

PROTEIN 1G

minty cucumber cooler

SERVES 2

1 cucumber, peeled and roughly chopped

2 tbsp. lemon juice

2 tbsp. fresh mint leaves

2 tbsp. agave

2 to 3 ice cubes

Place all ingredients in the Single Serve Cup. Blend until smooth. Serve right away.

CALORIES 72

FAT 0G

CHOL 0MG

SODIUM 2MG

CARB 18G

FIBER 1G

PROTEIN 1G

Juices & Smoothies

juiced jewels

SERVES 2

1 small beet, peeled, cut in chunks

½ carrot, cut in half

1 apple, cored

½ cup spinach, tightly packed

2 tsp. fresh lemon juice

1 cup water

4 to 6 ice cubes

Place all ingredients in the Pitcher and blend for 5 seconds. Increase the speed and blend until very smooth. Serve at once.

CALORIES 72

FAT 0G

CHOL 0MG

SODIUM 2MG

CARB 18G

FIBER 1G

PROTEIN 1G

star of india

SERVES 2

1 cup green tea, chilled

1 cup fresh papaya, cut into chunks

2 tbsp. agave

pinch ground cardamom

6 ice cubes

Place all ingredients in the Pitcher and blend until smooth. Serve at once.

Juices & Smoothies

morning oat smoothie

SERVES 1

½ cup steel cut oats, soaked overnight

½ frozen banana, peeled

2 tbsp. toasted almonds

2 tbsp. organic raisins

1 tbsp. agave

½ cup fat-free frozen vanilla yogurt

¼ cup water

Place all ingredients in the Single Serve Cup. Blend or pulse until smooth. Serve right away.

CALORIES 173

FAT 0G

CHOL 1MG

SODIUM 32MG

CARB 16G

FIBER 1G

PROTEIN 2G

berry, berry good day

SERVES 2 TO 3

½ cup fresh or frozen raspberries

¼ cup fresh or frozen strawberries, hulled

¼ cup fresh blueberries

¼ cup fresh pineapple chunks

1 tbsp. goji berries

½ cup low-fat plain yogurt

¼ cup water

6 to 8 ice cubes

Place all ingredients in the Pitcher and blend until smooth. Serve at once.

CALORIES 65

FAT 1G

CHOL 2MG

SODIUM 38MG

CARB 12G

FIBER 3G

PROTEIN 3G

banana coconut energizer

SERVES 2

½ cup fresh or frozen shredded coconut

1 frozen banana, peeled, cut in half

1 oz. dark chocolate

2 pitted dates

1 cup low-fat milk

2 to 3 ice cubes

Place all ingredients in the Single Serve Cup. Blend until smooth. Serve at once.

CALORIES 165

FAT 11G

CHOL 2MG

SODIUM 38MG

CARB 12G

FIBER 3G

PROTEIN 3G

breakfast smoothie for two

SERVES 2

1 banana, peeled and cut in half

1 cup frozen strawberries

½ cup frozen blueberries

½ cup liquid egg whites

½ cup low-fat plain yogurt

1 tbsp. honey

Place all ingredients in the Pitcher and blend until smooth. Serve at once.

CALORIES 175

FAT 1G

CHOL 4MG

SODIUM 69MG

CARB 38G

FIBER 4G

PROTEIN 6G

Juices & Smoothies

fresh rice milk

MAKES ABOUT 4 CUPS

1 cup cooked white or brown rice, cooled

4 cups water

1 tbsp. maple syrup or honey

½ tsp. pure vanilla extract

Place the cooled rice in the Pitcher and add 1 cup of water. Blend to make a medium paste. Add the remaining water, honey and extract and blend again until mixed. Blend on High for 10 seconds.

Line a large strainer with cheesecloth or a double layer of high-quality paper towels. Strain the milk over the lined strainer into a large pitcher or bowl. Gently stir the milk in the strainer with a spoon or spatula and press lightly until the all the liquid has been removed. Pour into a tightly sealed container and store in the refrigerator for up to 5 days.

CALORIES 51

FAT 0G

CHOL 0MG

SODIUM 0MG

CARB 11G

FIBER 0G

PROTEIN 0G

fresh coconut milk

MAKES 4 TO 5 CUPS

Meat from 2 coconuts, inner brown peel
removed
4½ cups warm water, divided

Place the coconut meat in the Pitcher and add 1 cup
water. Blend on High for about 30 seconds. Mixture
should resemble a medium paste. Add 1 cup water and
blend again for 10 seconds. Add the remaining water and
repeat.

Line a large strainer with cheesecloth or a double layer of
high-quality paper towels. Strain the milk over the lined
strainer into a large pitcher or bowl. Gently stir the milk
in the strainer with a spoon or spatula and press lightly
until the all the liquid has been removed. Set aside.

If thinner milk is desired, return the coconut meat to the
Pitcher and blend again, using 1 cup water. Repeat the
straining process and add the milk to the first batch. Store
the coconut milk in a tightly sealed container for 3-4 days.

fresh almond milk

MAKES 4 CUPS

1½ cups raw, blanched almonds (not roasted)

4-5 cups water, divided

2 tbsp. honey, divided

1 tsp. pure vanilla extract (optional)

pinch ground cinnamon (optional)

Place the almonds in the Pitcher and add enough water to cover. Blend until a smooth paste forms, about 10 seconds. Add 1 tbsp. honey, optional ingredients, and 2 cups water. Blend until the mixture is smooth.

Line a strainer with cheesecloth or a double layer of high-quality paper towels. Strain the milk over the lined strainer into a large pitcher or bowl. Gently stir the milk in the strainer with a spoon or spatula until the liquid has been removed. Set aside.

Spoon the remaining almond meal in the strainer back into the Pitcher again and add up to 1½ cups water. Add 1 tablespoon honey and blend on 3 for 10 seconds. Strain again as directed above. Combine with the first batch of milk and refrigerate in a tightly sealed container for up to 5 days.

CALORIES 45

FAT 2G

CHOL 0MG

SODIUM 113MG

CARB 6G

FIBER 1G

PROTEIN 1G

soups, sides, entrées & more!

The **NINJA** Kitchen System FLIP Cookbook

Pascoe Publishing, Inc.
Rocklin, CA

lemony sage white bean dip

SERVES 6 TO 8

1 15 oz. can white beans, drained,
        liquid reserved
1 clove garlic, peeled
1 tbsp. fresh sage leaves
2 tbsp. white wine
1 tbsp. lemon zest
¼ tsp. salt

Place all ingredients in the Bowl and blend until smooth. Serve at room temperature or chill slightly before serving.

CALORIES 48

FAT 0G

CHOL 0MG

SODIUM 49MG

CARB 3G

FIBER 0G

PROTEIN 0G

Soups, Sides, Entrées and More!

smokey sweet pepper dip with crostini

SERVES 6 TO 8

1 baguette bread, cut in ¼ inch slices

2 tbsp. olive oil

1 14 oz. can garbanzo beans, drained

4 oz. jarred roasted red peppers, drained

1 clove garlic, peeled

1 tbsp. balsamic vinegar

½ tsp. smoked Hungarian paprika

½ tsp. salt

¼ tsp. black pepper

Preheat the broiler to high. Lightly brush bread slices with oil on one side and place under the broiler pan, oiled side up. Broil until toasted and set aside.

Place all remaining ingredients into the Bowl and blend until smooth. Taste and adjust seasonings.

Serve in a small serving bowl placed in the center of a large platter and surrounded by the crostini.

CALORIES 116

FAT 4G

CHOL 0MG

SODIUM 358MG

CARB 17G

FIBER 3G

PROTEIN 3G

el paso mango-chile stuffed jalapeños

MAKES 12

½ peeled mango, roughly cut

1 4 oz. can diced green chiles

6 oz. low-fat cream cheese

1 tsp. lime juice

½ tsp. ground cumin

12 jalapeño peppers, halved and seeded

4 pieces bacon, cut in thirds

Preheat oven to 375°F. Place mango, chiles, cream cheese, lime juice and cumin into the Bowl and blend to combine.

Stuff mixture into jalapeño halves, wrap each with a piece of bacon and secure with a toothpick. Place on a parchment lined baking sheet and bake until bacon is crisp and filling is creamy and heated through, about 25 minutes. Serve warm or at room temperature.

CALORIES 5

FAT 3G

CHOL 7MG

SODIUM 77MG

CARB 7G

FIBER 1G

PROTEIN 3G

4

Soups, Sides, Entrées and More!

oven baked crab cakes

MAKES 12 TO 14 CAKES

2 stalks celery, with leaves, trimmed and
cut into 1-inch pieces

1 shallot, peeled and roughly cut

½ cup fresh parsley

1 clove garlic, peeled

2 tsp. olive oil

2 eggs, beaten

1 cup bread crumbs

2 tbsp. mayonnaise

2 tsp. Dijon mustard

1½ tsp. Old Bay Seasoning™

¼ tsp. salt

16 oz. lump crabmeat

Preheat oven to 400°F. Place celery, shallot, parsley and garlic in the Bowl and pulse to coarsely chop. In a non-stick sauté pan, heat oil over medium heat and sauté vegetables until softened.

Transfer vegetables to a mixing bowl and add remaining ingredients, gently mixing to combine. Shape mixture into round cakes about 1-inch thick and place on a parchment-lined baking sheet. Bake for about 20 minutes, until firm inside and golden outside.

CALORIES 79

FAT 3G

CHOL 57MG

SODIUM 320MG

CARB 6G

FIBER 1G

PROTEIN 6G

texas corn salsa

MAKES 3 CUPS

2 ripe tomatoes, cored

½ small onion, peeled

1 jalapeño pepper, seeded

2 tbsp. fresh cilantro leaves

2 tbsp. lime juice

2 tsp. red wine vinegar

½ tsp. cumin seeds

½ tsp. salt

½ tsp. black pepper

½ cup fresh corn kernels

½ cup cooked black beans, no liquid

CALORIES 12

FAT 0G

CHOL 0MG

SODIUM 90MG

CARB 2G

FIBER 1G

PROTEIN 1G

Place tomatoes, onion, jalapeño, cilantro, lime juice, vinegar, cumin, salt and pepper in the Bowl and pulse to chop until just chunky. Transfer to a serving bowl and stir in corn and beans. Serve with chips or over grilled fish.

Soups, Sides, Entrées and More!

spicy shrimp potstickers with peanut dipping sauce

MAKES 24 POTSTICKERS, 2 PER SERVING

2 carrots, cut horizontally then into 1-inch pieces
¼ napa cabbage, core removed
2 green onions, trimmed and roughly cut
2 tbsp. fresh cilantro leaves
¼ cup roasted peanuts
1 tsp. fresh ginger
¼ tsp. chile garlic sauce
1 tsp. toasted sesame oil
½ tsp. salt
½ lb. shrimp, cooked, peeled and partially frozen
24 wonton wrappers
4 tsp. oil, divided
2 tbsp. water

DIPPING SAUCE:
½ cup roasted peanuts
¼ cup water
3 tbsp. soy sauce
1 tbsp. mirin

½ tsp. agave
½ tsp. chile garlic sauce

Place carrots, cabbage, onion, cilantro, peanuts and ginger in the Bowl and pulse to chop. Place in a large bowl. Place the sauce, oil, salt, and shrimp in the Bowl and pulse to chop. Add to the cabbage mixture and toss.

Place a teaspoon of filling in the center of each wonton and fold over to form a triangle, sealing the edges lightly with water to seal. Heat 2 teaspoons oil over medium-high heat. Cook one half of the potstickers until browned. Add water to the pan, cover and simmer for 4 minutes. Uncover and cook until liquid is gone. Repeat with the remaining potstickers.

Place the Dipping Sauce ingredients in the Single Serve Cup and pulse until smooth. Pass the sauce with the potstickers.

Soups, Sides, Entrées and More!

CALORIES 129

FAT 7G

CHOL 22MG

SODIUM 502MG

CARB 10G

FIBER 2G

PROTEIN 8G

garlic roasted potato wedges

SERVES 6 TO 8

4-6 russet potatoes, scrubbed and cut
    into wedges
6 cloves garlic, peeled
6 chives, roughly cut
¼ cup olive oil
2 tsp. salt
1 tsp. black pepper

CALORIES 69

FAT 7G

CHOL 1MG

SODIUM 588MG

CARB 2G

FIBER 2G

PROTEIN 2G

Preheat oven to 425°F. Place garlic, chives and oil in the Single Serve Cup and pulse to chop and blend. Toss potato wedges with garlic mixture, salt and pepper and place on a baking sheet and roast for 20 minutes. Use a spatula to stir potatoes and roast for 15 to 20 minutes longer until crisp and golden browned. Serve while warm.

Soups, Sides, Entrées and More!

italian bruschetta with creamy balsamic spread

SERVES 6 TO 8

1 baguette, sliced into ¼ inch-thick rounds

¼ cup extra virgin olive oil

6 oz. can sliced black olives, divided

14 oz. can garbanzo beans, drained

1 tbsp. balsamic vinegar

¼ tsp. red pepper flakes

1 clove garlic, peeled

1 tsp. salt

¼ tsp. ground black pepper

2 tbsp. flat-leaf parsley, chopped, for garnish

Preheat the broiler to High. Brush each baguette slice generously with olive oil on one side and place on the broiler pan, oiled side up. Broil until toasted and set aside.

Place one-half of the olives and the remaining ingredients, except the parsley, in the Bowl. Pulse until smooth. To serve, spoon a small amount of the balsamic spread on each toast and garnish with the remaining sliced olives and parsley.

CALORIES 265

FAT 8G

CHOL 0MG

SODIUM 1,064MG

CARB 44G

FIBER 5G

PROTEIN 8G

smoked salmon spread

SERVES 8

8 oz. low fat cream cheese, at room temperature

¼ cup low fat sour cream

¼ cup low fat Greek yogurt

1 tbsp. fresh lemon juice

2 tsp. fresh dill, plus more for garnish

2 tsp. chives (or green onions), plus more for garnish

½ tsp. salt

¼ tsp. ground black pepper

4 oz. smoked salmon, roughly chopped

thinly sliced rye bread rounds

Place the cream cheese, sour cream, yogurt, lemon juice, dill, chives, salt, pepper, and half of the smoked salmon in the Bowl. Pulse until smooth.

Place the spread in a serving dish and mix in the remaining salmon by hand. Garnish with dill and chives, if desired. Serve right away with rye bread rounds or chill until serving.

CALORIES 95

FAT 6G

CHOL 20MG

SODIUM 347MG

CARB 3G

FIBER 0G

PROTEIN 7G

Soups, Sides, Entrées and More!

pineapple & red onion salsa

SERVES 6 TO 8

¼ cup red onion, roughly cut

3 tbsp. fresh cilantro leaves

2 cups fresh pineapple, roughly cut

1 tbsp. raw, unfiltered honey

2 tbsp. fresh lime juice

Place all the ingredients in the Bowl and pulse quickly, just until chunky. Serve right away over mild white fish or poultry.

CALORIES 49

FAT 0G

CHOL 0MG

SODIUM 2MG

CARB 14G

FIBER 1G

PROTEIN 0G

cherry tomato bites

MAKES 24 APPETIZERS

24 large cherry tomatoes
1 large ripe avocado, seeded and skin removed
4 oz. feta cheese, crumbled
1 tbsp. lemon juice
3 tbsp. chives
salt to taste

CALORIES 124

FAT 9G

CHOL 17MG

SODIUM 239MG

CARB 8G

FIBER 2G

PROTEIN 3G

Position the Dough Blade in the Bowl. Slice ¼-inch off the bottom of each tomato, reserving the slices. Remove the juice, seeds, and flesh from the inside of each cherry tomato. Set aside, stem side down.

Place the remaining ingredients in the Bowl. Pulse until smooth.

Place 1 teaspoon of the avocado mixture into each cherry tomato. Top each with a reserved tomato slice.

Soups, Sides, Entrées and More!

east indian spiced lentil dip with naan bread

SERVES 3 TO 4

1 tbsp. fresh lemon juice

1 tbsp. extra virgin olive oil

¼ tsp. ground cumin

⅛ tsp. ground coriander

¼ tsp. salt

⅛ tsp. ground black pepper

1½ cups red lentils, cooked

¼ sweet onion, roughly cut

2 cloves garlic, peeled

½ jalapeño pepper, seeded, roughly cut

1 or 2 Indian naan breads, torn into
     bite-sized pieces

Place the juice, oil, cumin, coriander, salt and pepper in the Bowl. Pulse 3 times. Add the lentils, onion, garlic and pepper. Pulse until smooth. Chill very well before serving with the bread.

CALORIES 206

FAT 6G

CHOL 0MG

SODIUM 148MG

CARB 30G

FIBER 6G

PROTEIN 7G

duxelle cucumber cups

MAKES 16 APPETIZERS

1 lb. fresh cremini mushrooms, trimmed

1 clove garlic, peeled

1 tsp. fresh thyme leaves

1 tsp. lemon zest

1 tbsp. extra virgin olive oil

½ tsp. salt

¼ tsp. ground black pepper

2 seedless, thin-skinned English cucumbers

¼ cup crème fraiche (or use sour cream, if desired)

parsley for garnish (optional)

CALORIES 91

FAT 3G

CHOL 3MG

SODIUM 1,216MG

CARB 7G

FIBER 2G

PROTEIN 2G

Place the mushrooms, garlic, thyme and lemon zest in the Bowl and pulse until the mixture is chunky. In a large pan over medium-high heat, sauté the mushroom mixture in the olive oil for about 5 minutes, allowing the excess liquid to cook off. Add salt and pepper and let cool.

Meanwhile, peel the cucumber partially, so it still has strips of skin. Trim the ends off the cucumbers and cut each cucumber into slices 1-inch thick. Scoop out the center of each slice with a melon baller, forming a cup of flesh. Fill the cucumber cup with 1 teaspoon of the mushroom mixture. Top each with a dollop of crème fraiche and garnish with parsley leaves.

Soups, Sides, Entrées and More!

bacon & cheddar stuffed boule

SERVES 8

6 slices crisp cooked bacon, plus more for garnish

¼ red onion, peeled, roughly cut

1 sprig rosemary, removed from stalk, plus more
     for garnish

4 oz. extra sharp cheddar cheese, cut into
     1 ounce sticks

1 tbsp. balsamic vinegar

½ cup low fat plain Greek yogurt

8 oz. low fat cream cheese

1 boule sourdough bread (round bread loaf)

Preheat the oven to 350°F.

Place all ingredients, except the bread, in the Bowl and pulse until smooth. Slice off the top of the sourdough round and remove most of the bread center, reserving the bread inside. Fill the center of the boule with the dip and cover with the top slice. Wrap in foil and bake for 50 minutes. Unwrap and bake for an additional 10 minutes.

Cut the bread pieces into rough cubes and arrange around the boule. Garnish with additional bacon and rosemary.

CALORIES 253

FAT 7G

CHOL 13MG

SODIUM 563MG

CARB 33G

FIBER 1G

PROTEIN 15G

chilled jumbo shrimp with sweet chili dipping sauce

SERVES 3 TO 4

1 lb. extra large shrimp, cooked, shelled,
    deveined, with tails

¼ cup rice wine vinegar

2 tbsp. fish sauce

¼ cup hot water

2 tbsp. sugar

1 tbsp. fresh lime juice

½ clove garlic

1 tsp. Asian red chili paste (such as sambal)

Place the shrimp over ice in a serving bowl and keep well-chilled.

Combine all remaining ingredients in the Single Serve Cup and pulse until smooth. Serve the shrimp with the sauce right away. Chill any leftovers.

CALORIES 54

FAT 0G

CHOL 43MG

SODIUM 753MG

CARB 7G

FIBER 0G

PROTEIN 5G

Soups, Sides, Entrées and More!

green goddess dip with tender crisp green beans

SERVES 6

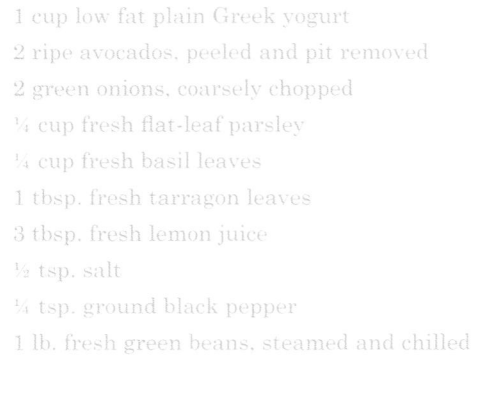

1 cup low fat plain Greek yogurt

2 ripe avocados, peeled and pit removed

2 green onions, coarsely chopped

¼ cup fresh flat-leaf parsley

¼ cup fresh basil leaves

1 tbsp. fresh tarragon leaves

3 tbsp. fresh lemon juice

½ tsp. salt

¼ tsp. ground black pepper

1 lb. fresh green beans, steamed and chilled

Place all the ingredients, except the beans, in the Bowl and pulse until very smooth. Spoon the dip into a serving bowl and serve right away with the green beans for dipping.

CALORIES 162

FAT 10G

CHOL 2MG

SODIUM 219MG

CARB 13G

FIBER 7G

PROTEIN 7G

Soups, Sides, Entrées and More!

island butternut squash soup

SERVES 4

3 cloves garlic, peeled
2 tbsp. fresh ginger, peeled
1 jalapeño pepper, seeded
1 medium yellow onion, peeled, roughly cut
4 lbs. butternut squash, cooked, cubed and cooled
3 cups sodium-reduced chicken or vegetable broth
1 tsp. salt (or to taste)
1 tbsp. brown sugar (optional)

CALORIES 70

FAT 0G

CHOL 0MG

SODIUM 999MG

CARB 15G

FIBER 3G

PROTEIN 3G

Place the garlic, ginger, pepper and onion in the Bowl and pulse until finely chopped. Set aside.

Working in batches, pulse the butternut squash in the Bowl and add broth to create a pourable puree. Pour the pureed squash into a large saucepot and add the chopped vegetables. Repeat with the remaining squash. Slowly add the remaining broth, whisking together to combine. Season with salt and sugar as desired. Heat on medium until simmering and ready to serve, about 8 minutes.

18

Soups, Sides, Entrées and More!

roasted vegetable bisque

SERVES 4

6 cups roasted root vegetables (broccoli, asparagus, squash, sweet potato, cauliflower, etc.), cooled

1 tbsp. fresh chives

1 tbsp . flat-leaf parsley

3 cups sodium-reduced chicken or vegetable broth, divided

½ cup low fat milk (or cream, if desired)

1 tsp. salt (or to taste)

1 tsp. ground black pepper

Place about one-third of the vegetables and herbs in the Bowl and add one-half cup of broth. Pulse until pureed and smooth. Spoon the puree into a saucepot and repeat with the remaining roasted vegetables and herbs.

Add the remaining broth and milk, mixing well, and heat on medium until just simmering. Season with salt and pepper to taste, and continue simmering for about 10 minutes.

CALORIES 115

FAT 1G

CHOL 1MG

SODIUM 886MG

CARB 24G

FIBER 6G

PROTEIN 11G

spiced carrot apple soup with toasted hazelnuts

SERVES 4

2 cups carrots, peeled, roughly cut

1 medium ripe Gala apple, peeled, roughly cut

¼-inch piece fresh ginger, peeled

1 tsp. ground cinnamon

3 cups reduced-sodium chicken or vegetable broth

½ cup hazelnuts, skins removed

1 tbsp. butter

CALORIES 132

FAT 7G

CHOL 8MG

SODIUM 481MG

CARB 14G

FIBER 4G

PROTEIN 4G

Place the carrots in the Bowl and pulse until finely chopped. Spoon the carrots into a saucepot and set aside. Place the apple, ginger and cinnamon in the Bowl and pulse until finely chopped. Add the mixture to the carrots in the saucepot. Add the broth to the carrot/apple mixture and heat on medium until warm and simmering, about 8 minutes.

Meanwhile, place the hazelnuts in the Bowl and pulse until chopped. Remove and sauté the nuts in the butter on medium heat until lightly toasted and fragrant, about 2 minutes. To serve, ladle the warm soup into bowls and top with the toasted hazelnuts.

Soups, Sides, Entrées and More!

spicy black bean soup

SERVES 4

2 14 oz. cans black beans, drained
1 jalapeño pepper, seeded, roughly cut
1 ripe tomato, roughly cut
½ lime, juiced
¼ white onion, peeled, roughly cut
2 cloves garlic, peeled
¼ red pepper, seeded, roughly cut
¼ cup fresh cilantro, loosely packed
salt and pepper to taste

Place all of the ingredients in the Bowl and pulse until smooth. Heat briefly or serve at room temperature.

CALORIES 184

FAT 1G

CHOL 0MG

SODIUM 696MG

CARB 37G

FIBER 12G

PROTEIN 13G

Soups, Sides, Entrées and More!

duo tomato gazpacho

SERVES 4

1 slice stale white bread, roughly torn

6 plum tomatoes, halved

1 medium seedless cucumber, peeled and quartered

1 bell pepper, cored and seeded, quartered

1 clove garlic, peeled

2 tbsp. red wine vinegar

1 tsp. salt (or to taste)

½ tsp. ground black pepper

1 cup tomato juice (plus 1 cup, to taste)

CALORIES 55

FAT 0G

CHOL 0MG

SODIUM 954MG

CARB 12G

FIBER 2G

PROTEIN 3G

Pulse the bread in the Bowl until crumbed. Place in a large serving bowl. Place 3 tomatoes in the Bowl and pulse until smooth. Pour into the serving bowl with the crumbs. Repeat with the remaining tomatoes. Pulse the bell pepper and garlic and add to the tomatoes and crumbs.

Add the vinegar, salt and pepper to taste, plus the tomato juice to taste. Stir well and chill until serving.

Soups, Sides, Entrées and More!

spring asparagus soup with crème fraiche

SERVES 4

1 large leek, green leaves removed

1 tbsp. extra virgin olive oil

1 lb. asparagus spears, woody ends removed

2¼ cups reduced sodium chicken or vegetable
    broth, divided

1½ cups spring peas (fresh or frozen)

1 cup low fat plain yogurt

3 fresh mint leaves

½ cup crème fraiche for garnish (optional)

Place the leek in the Single Serve Cup and pulse until chopped. Heat the oil on medium-high in a large saucepot and sauté the leek for 5 minutes. Add the asparagus spears and 1 cup broth and bring to a boil. Reduce to a simmer, cover, and cook about 3 minutes. Add the peas. After another minute, remove from heat and let cool.

Working in batches, place the cooled mixture in the Bowl with the yogurt and mint leaves. Pulse until smooth. Pour into a serving bowl and add the remaining broth. Stir well and chill before serving. Garnish with a dollop of crème fraiche.

CALORIES 269

FAT 16G

CHOL 44MG

SODIUM 605MG

CARB 22G

FIBER 6G

PROTEIN 9G

roasted garlic & roma tomato soup

SERVES 4

2½ lbs. fresh Roma tomatoes, sliced in
    half lengthwise
1 medium yellow onion, peeled and cut into
    quarters
8 cloves garlic, peeled
3 tbsp. extra virgin olive oil
½ tsp. salt
¼ tsp. ground black pepper
1 cup tomato juice
1 cup half-and-half cream
1 tbsp. fresh basil leaves, chopped
1 cup high-quality croutons for garnish

Preheat the oven to 375°F. Place the tomatoes, onion, and garlic in a single layer on a baking pan. Avoid over-crowding the vegetables. Drizzle with the olive oil and season with salt and pepper. Roast for 45 minutes, turning once or twice. Remove from the oven and let cool.

Working in batches, place the roasted vegetables in the Bowl. Pulse each batch until smooth. Spoon into a large saucepan and add the tomato juice, cream and basil. Adjust the seasonings to taste. Warm over medium-low heat for about 5 minutes until barely simmering. Do not boil. Serve in 4 bowls with croutons to garnish.

CALORIES 286

FAT 20G

CHOL 24MG

SODIUM 513MG

CARB 25G

FIBER 5G

PROTEIN 6G

Soups, Sides, Entrées and More!

baby spinach salad with champagne honey vinaigrette

SERVES 4 TO 6

6 cups baby spinach leaves

8 cremini mushrooms, sliced and sautéed

¼ small red onion, peeled, roughly cut

2 tbsp. champagne vinegar

2 tbsp. extra virgin olive oil

2 tbsp. raw, unfiltered honey

1 tsp. salt

½ tsp. ground black pepper

4 tbsp. crumbled feta cheese, for garnish

In a large mixing bowl, combine the spinach leaves and mushrooms. Set aside.

Place the red onion in the Single Serve Cup and pulse until chopped. Add the onion to the spinach and mushrooms. Place the vinegar, oil, honey, salt and pepper in the Single Serve Cup and pulse to blend. Drizzle the vinaigrette over the salad to taste. Garnish each serving with a sprinkling of feta cheese.

CALORIES 138

FAT 9G

CHOL 9MG

SODIUM 724MG

CARB 9G

FIBER 1G

PROTEIN 4G

Soups, Sides, Entrées and More!

super green sunflower salad

SERVES 4

½ bunch dark green kale, ribs removed, torn into
    bite-sized pieces

1 bunch Swiss chard, ribs removed, torn into
    bite-sized pieces

½ small red onion, peeled, roughly cut

½ carrot, peeled, roughly cut

½ cup canned mandarin orange segments

1 tbsp. orange juice

1 tbsp. rice vinegar

1 tsp. sesame oil

1 tbsp. tamari (or soy sauce/low-sodium soy sauce)

½ tsp. sugar

¼ cup salted sunflower seeds

Place the kale and Swiss chard in a large serving bowl. Place the onion and carrots in the Bowl and pulse to chop evenly. Spoon the vegetables over the greens and add the mandarin oranges.

Place the remaining ingredients, except the sunflower seeds, in the Bowl and pulse until blended. Pour over the salad, add the seeds, and toss well to combine. Chill before serving.

Soups, Sides, Entrées and More!

bok choy salad with cashew dressing

SERVES 4

6 cups raw bok choy, chopped

2 fresh carrots, peeled, roughly cut

2 stalks celery, roughly cut

3 green onions, cut in half

½ cup unsalted toasted cashews, divided

1 tbsp. fresh lemon juice

1 tsp. tamari (or soy sauce/low sodium soy sauce)

3 tbsp. flaxseed oil

½ tsp. salt

½ tsp. ground black pepper

Spoon the bok choy into a serving bowl. Place the carrots, celery and green onions in the Bowl and pulse until finely chopped and add the mixture to the bok choy.

Place one-fourth cup cashews, lemon juice, tamari, flaxseed oil, salt and black pepper in the Bowl and pulse until blended. Pour the dressing over the salad and toss well to combine. Garnish each serving with the remaining toasted cashews.

CALORIES 221

FAT 19G

CHOL 0MG

SODIUM 455MG

CARB 11G

FIBER 2G

PROTEIN 5G

Soups, Sides, Entrées and More!

orange fennel salad

SERVES 4

2 large fennel bulbs, fronds discarded, sliced

2 fresh oranges, peeled, segmented

½ small red onion, peeled, quartered

1 tbsp. flat leaf parsley

2 tbsp. fresh orange juice

1 tbsp. fresh lemon juice

3 tbsp. extra virgin olive oil

½ tsp. salt

½ tsp. ground black pepper

Place the fennel and orange segments in a large mixing bowl.

Place the onion, parsley, orange juice, lemon juice, olive oil, salt, and pepper in the Single Serve Cup and pulse until the onion is evenly chopped. Pour the dressing over the salad and toss well to combine. Serve right away or chill.

CALORIES 175

FAT 11G

CHOL 0MG

SODIUM 352MG

CARB 21G

FIBER 6G

PROTEIN 2G

Soups, Sides, Entrées and More!

asian shrimp slaw with ginger sesame vinaigrette

SERVES 4

6 cups Napa (savoy) cabbage leaves, thinly sliced

1 large red bell pepper, seeded, quartered

1 tsp. fresh ginger

1 cup snow peas, thinly sliced

2 cups cooked large shrimp, without shells

3 tbsp. rice wine vinegar

2 tsp. sesame oil

1 tsp. soy sauce (or low sodium soy sauce)

2 tbsp. extra virgin olive oil

1 tbsp. toasted sesame seeds

salt and pepper to taste

Place the cabbage in a serving bowl. Place the red pepper and ginger in the Single Serve Cup and pulse to chop. Add to the cabbage. Add the snow peas and shrimp to the cabbage.

Place the rice wine vinegar, sesame oil, soy sauce and olive oil in the Single Serve Cup and pulse until blended. Pour the dressing over the salad and toss well to combine. Add salt and pepper to taste and serve right away. Top with the sesame seeds just before serving.

CALORIES 188

FAT 6G

CHOL 220MG

SODIUM 313MG

CARB 9G

FIBER 3G

PROTEIN 27G

mexican chicken salad with chipotle lime dressing

SERVES 4

1 cup cooked chicken, shredded
1 cup cooked black beans
1 cup corn kernels (frozen or canned)
4 cups romaine lettuce, shredded
1 large tomato, quartered
1 tbsp. fresh cilantro leaves
2 green onions, roughly cut
1 chipotle pepper in adobo sauce
½ cup low fat plain yogurt
1 tsp. fresh lime juice
½ tsp. salt
¼ tsp. ground black pepper

Place the chicken, black beans, corn and lettuce in a large serving bowl.

Place the tomato, cilantro and green onions in the Single Serve Cup and pulse once or twice to evenly chop. Add the tomato mixture to the chicken and lettuce.

Place the pepper, yogurt, lime juice, salt and pepper in the Single Serve Cup and pulse until smooth. Pour the dressing over the salad and toss lightly. Serve at once.

CALORIES 189

FAT 2G

CHOL 32MG

SODIUM 583MG

CARB 25G

FIBER 6G

PROTEIN 17G

30

Soups, Sides, Entrées and More!

chicken caesar salad

SERVES 4 TO 5

2 boneless, skinless chicken breasts,
    grilled and sliced

6 cups romaine lettuce, torn

½ cup silken tofu

¼ cup buttermilk

2 tbsp. fresh lemon juice

1 tbsp. white wine vinegar

2 tsp. Dijon mustard

1 clove garlic, peeled

2 canned anchovies

1 cup seasoned salad croutons

¼ cup Parmesan cheese, shaved

In a large mixing bowl, combine the chicken slices and the lettuce. Set aside.

In the Single Serve Cup, place the tofu, buttermilk, lemon juice, vinegar, mustard, garlic and anchovies. Pulse until creamy. Pour the dressing over the salad to taste and toss to coat. Add the croutons and Parmesan cheese just prior to serving.

CALORIES 190

FAT 7G

CHOL 37MG

SODIUM 398MG

CARB 16G

FIBER 2G

PROTEIN 16G

Soups, Sides, Entrées and More!

old el paso chicken with toasted pumpkin mole sauce

SERVES 4

CALORIES 526

FAT 12G

CHOL 96MG

SODIUM 947MG

CARB 57G

FIBER 4G

PROTEIN 45G

1 cup hulled pumpkin seeds, toasted

1 small white onion, roughly cut

3 cloves garlic, peeled

¼ cup fresh cilantro leaves, plus more for garnish

2 romaine lettuce leaves, roughly torn

½ serrano pepper, seeded

½ tsp. ground cumin

2½ cups chicken or vegetable broth, plus
     1 cup as needed

1 tbsp. canola oil

1 tsp. salt

4 small boneless, skinless chicken breasts

4 to 6 cups brown rice, steamed and kept warm

cilantro for garnish, optional

Place the pumpkin seeds, onion, garlic, cilantro, lettuce, pepper and cumin in the Bowl. Add ½ cup broth and pulse until smooth. Add ½ cup broth and pulse again briefly.

In a large skillet, heat the oil on medium-high heat. Add the blender mixture to the skillet and cook until very thick. Whisk in the remaining 1½ cups of chicken broth and add the salt and chicken. Add up to 1 cup additional broth, if desired. Bring to a boil and reduce to a simmer; cook for 8 minutes or until chicken is cooked through and no pink remains.

To serve, divide the rice between 4 dinner plates and top with the chicken and sauce. Garnish with cilantro, if desired.

Soups, Sides, Entrées and More!

new orleans chicken & shrimp jambalaya

SERVES 4

2 cloves garlic, peeled

1 small white onion, peeled and roughly cut

½ cup green bell pepper, seeded and roughly cut

1 cup canned fire-roasted diced tomatoes, with juices

1 tsp. Cajun seasoning

½ tsp. Tabasco® sauce

2 cups chicken broth

1 cup long grain white rice (or quick-cooking brown rice)

½ lb. cooked chicken thigh meat, cut into bite-sized pieces

½ lb. medium shrimp, peeled, deveined

salt and pepper to taste

Place the garlic, onion, green pepper, tomatoes, seasoning and Tabasco® sauce in the Bowl and pulse just until chopped. Spoon into a large sauté pan and add the broth and rice. Bring to a boil on high heat; cover and reduce to a simmer for 20 minutes. Add the chicken and shrimp and cook for about 5 minutes until the shrimp are cooked through. Adjust seasonings to taste before serving.

CALORIES 320

FAT 11G

CHOL 81MG

SODIUM 567MG

CARB 30G

FIBER 4G

PROTEIN 11G

sesame chicken lo mein

SERVES 4

1 clove garlic, chopped
½ small white onion, chopped
2 tbsp. canola oil, divided
1 red bell pepper, seeded, cut in strips
4 small boneless, skinless chicken breasts,
    cut in strips
1 tsp. sesame oil
¼ cup tamari (or use low sodium soy sauce)
2 tbsp. creamy peanut butter
¼ tsp. ground black pepper
½ lb. spaghetti noodles, cooked, kept warm
2 tbsp. fresh cilantro leaves, chopped
2 tbsp. peanuts, chopped

Sauté the garlic and onion in the canola oil over medium-high heat. Add the red pepper and chicken and reduce the heat to medium. Sauté for about 5 minutes, or until the chicken is no longer pink.

Meanwhile, pulse the sesame oil, tamari, peanut butter and black pepper in the Single Serve Cup until smooth. Stir into the chicken and peppers and heat through.

To serve, toss the chicken and peppers with the noodles and garnish with the cilantro and peanuts before serving.

CALORIES 511

FAT 23G

CHOL 96MG

SODIUM 785MG

CARB 30G

FIBER 3G

PROTEIN 40G

Soups, Sides, Entrées and More!

oven baked walnut pesto-crusted halibut

SERVES 6

¼ cup toasted walnuts

2 cups packed basil leaves

½ cup Parmesan cheese, cut in chunks

½ tsp. salt

½ tsp. black pepper

¼ cup olive oil

6 halibut steaks, 1-inch thick

Place walnuts, basil, cheese, salt and pepper in the Pitcher and blend until combined. With motor running, drizzle oil through pour spout and blend until smooth.

Preheat oven to 450°F. Place fish on a parchment lined baking sheet. Spread top of each steak with a generous amount of pesto and bake for 12 to 14 minutes, or until crust is crispy and fish is cooked through. Refrigerate any unused pesto sauce and use within 3 days.

CALORIES 341

FAT 23G

CHOL 41MG

SODIUM 347MG

CARB 4G

FIBER 1G

PROTEIN 29G

grilled salmon with maple dijon sauce

SERVES 4

2 tbsp. extra virgin olive oil

2 tbsp. Dijon mustard

1 tbsp. pure maple syrup

1 tbsp. fresh parsley leaves

1 clove garlic, peeled

½ tsp. salt

¼ tsp. ground black pepper

4 8 oz. salmon fillets, with skin

Preheat a grill to medium-high heat. In the Single Serve Cup, place the olive oil, mustard, syrup, parsley, garlic, salt and pepper. Pulse until smooth. Set aside one-half of the Dijon sauce. Brush the remaining half over the salmon fillets.

Grill the salmon over medium-high heat, 4 to 5 minutes on each side. Remove from grill and let rest for 5 minutes. Brush with the remaining sauce.

Soups, Sides, Entrées and More!

baja fish tacos

SERVES 4 TO 6

½ cup fresh cilantro leaves

1 lime, juiced

1 tbsp. raw, unfiltered honey

½ cup low fat mayonnaise

¼ red cabbage, thinly sliced

salt and black pepper to taste

3 tbsp. canola oil

12 small fresh corn tortillas

1 lb. white fish fillets, cut into bite-sized pieces

1 avocado, chopped

½ cup fresh prepared salsa

Place the cilantro, lime juice, honey and mayonnaise in the Bowl and pulse until smooth. Place the cabbage in a large mixing bowl and spoon the dressing over, tossing lightly to mix. Season with the salt and pepper to taste. Chill.

In a large sauté pan, heat the oil until shimmering. Using tongs, quickly dip the tortillas into the oil just until the tortillas are softened. Drain the tortillas on paper towels. Remove all but 1 tablespoon of oil from the pan and heat on medium. Add the fish and sauté, stirring often, until slightly crispy and cooked through. Set aside and keep warm.

To assemble, place a spoonful of the cabbage slaw in one tortilla, top with a few pieces of fish and add the avocado and salsa. Repeat with the remaining tacos. Serve right away.

CALORIES 364

FAT 12G

CHOL 50MG

SODIUM 383MG

CARB 43G

FIBER 8G

PROTEIN 24G

beef flank steak with chimichurri sauce

SERVES 6

1 ½ lb. beef flank steak
salt and pepper for seasoning
1 cup fresh Italian parsley, packed
½ cup extra virgin olive oil
⅓ cup red wine vinegar
¼ cup fresh cilantro, packed
2 cloves garlic, peeled
¾ tsp. dried crushed red pepper
½ tsp. ground cumin
½ tsp. salt

Preheat the oven to 450°F. Place the steak in a roasting pan and season with salt and pepper. Roast for 15 minutes, reduce the heat to 350°F and roast for another 15 to 20 minutes, until the internal temperature of the meat reaches 125°F. Remove from the oven and let rest for 15 minutes. Slice thinly across the grain and keep warm.

Meanwhile, in the Bowl, pulse the remaining ingredients until smooth. To serve, fan the steak slices on a serving platter and drizzle with the Chimichurri Sauce.

Soups, Sides, Entrées and More!

cranberry-mustard roasted pork loin

SERVES 6

14 oz. canned whole cranberry sauce

3 tbsp. Dijon mustard

1 shallot, peeled, roughly cut (or use ½ small
    white onion)

1 tbsp. red wine vinegar

1 tbsp. raw, unfiltered honey

1 tbsp. fresh rosemary leaves

2½ lbs. boneless pork loin

salt and pepper to taste

Preheat oven to 475°F. Place the cranberry sauce, mustard, shallot, vinegar, honey, and rosemary in the Bowl. Pulse until smooth. Reserve half of the sauce.

Place the pork loin in a heavy roasting pan. Season with salt and pepper. Cover the loin with half of the sauce. Place in the oven and roast for 30-40 minutes, until internal temperature has reached 140°F. Remove from the oven and let rest 15 minutes. Serve with the reserved half of the cranberry sauce.

CALORIES 350

FAT 11G

CHOL 92MG

SODIUM 101MG

CARB 28G

FIBER 1G

PROTEIN 32G

Soups, Sides, Entrées and More!

tender-crisp broccoli with fresh herb sauce

SERVES 4

1 lb. broccoli florets, steamed and blanched, warm
1 cup watercress leaves, tightly packed
1 cup low fat plain yogurt
¼ cup low fat mayonnaise
2 tbsp. fresh dill
2 tbsp. fresh basil leaves
2 tbsp. fresh mint leaves
1 green onion, roughly cut
1 tsp. red wine vinegar
½ tsp. salt

Place the broccoli florets in a serving bowl.

Place the remaining ingredients in the Bowl and pulse until smooth. Pour over the broccoli florets and toss to coat. Serve while warm or chill before serving.

CALORIES 72

FAT 2G

CHOL 4MG

SODIUM 479MG

CARB 9G

FIBER 0G

PROTEIN 3G

Soups, Sides, Entrées and More!

tomatoes gremolata

SERVES 4

4 large beefsteak tomatoes, cored, seeded and
cut in-half crosswise
salt and pepper for seasoning
5 slices stale bread
3 green onions, roughly cut
12 fresh basil leaves
½ cup flat leaf parsley leaves
2 cloves garlic, peeled
1 tbsp. lemon zest
extra virgin olive oil
¼ cup Gruyere cheese, grated

Preheat the oven to 400°F. Place the tomatoes in a
9 x 13-inch casserole dish and season with salt and
pepper. Place the bread, onions, basil, parsley, garlic,
and lemon zest in the Bowl and pulse until a bread

crumb mixture is formed. Divide among the tomato
halves, filling each tomato half compactly.

Drizzle each tomato with a little olive oil. Bake for
15 minutes. Top with the cheese and bake for an
additional few minutes until the cheese has melted.

CALORIES 80

FAT 3G

CHOL 8MG

SODIUM 106MG

CARB 11G

FIBER 2G

PROTEIN 4G

italian tiramisu parfaits

SERVES 4

8 oz. mascarpone cheese
2 tbsp. sugar
2 tbsp. brandy
1 pkg. ladyfingers
1½ cups strong coffee
1 cup whipped cream
toasted almonds
shaved chocolate

Position the Dough Blade in the Bowl. Place the cheese, sugar and brandy in the Bowl and pulse until smooth.

To assemble 4 parfaits, spoon a small amount of the cheese mixture in each of 4 wide glasses. Dip 2 ladyfingers into the coffee and place on top of the

Repeat with another layer of cheese to each parfait and repeat with the ladyfingers. Repeat the layers until the ingredients are used. Add a dollop of whipped cream to each parfait. Finish each with toasted almonds and shaved chocolate. Serve at once.

42

Soups, Sides, Entrées and More!

fresh fruit & lemon cream tart

SERVES 10

16 oz. low fat cream cheese (or use Neuchatel cheese), softened

⅓ cup sugar

1 lemon, juiced

1 refrigerated pie pastry, baked and cooled

2½ pints fresh fruit, such as berries, kiwi or stone fruit (sliced)

1 cup currant jelly, melted (or use other fruit jelly)

Position the Dough Paddle in the Bowl and add the cream cheese, sugar and lemon juice. Pulse until smooth.

Spoon the cream cheese mixture evenly onto the cooled pastry and smooth the top with a knife. Arrange the fruit in concentric circles over the cheese mixture and brush with the melted jelly. Chill to set.

CALORIES 406

FAT 18G

CHOL 85MG

SODIUM 210MG

CARB 55G

FIBER 2G

PROTEIN 10G

Soups, Sides, Entrées and More!

strawberry basil ice cream

MAKES 1 QUART

2 cups strawberries, stemmed and hulled
1 cup sugar
15 fresh basil leaves
2 cups whole milk
2 cups light cream
2 tsp. vanilla extract

Place the strawberries, sugar and basil in the Bowl.
Pulse until the strawberry mixture is smooth. Spoon
into a large bowl, add the remaining ingredients and
stir to combine.

Pour the ice cream mixture into the freezer bowl or
tub of your ice cream maker and proceed as directed.

CALORIES 225

FAT 9G

CHOL 29MG

SODIUM 50MG

CARB 34G

FIBER 1G

PROTEIN 4G

Soups, Sides, Entrées and More!

creamy dreamy cheesecake

SERVES 12

10 graham crackers
¼ cup sugar
¼ cup butter
2 8 oz. pkgs. low fat cream cheese, softened
1 cup mascarpone cheese
1 tbsp. fresh lemon juice
1 cup whipped cream
¼ cup sugar

Prepare crust by placing the crackers, sugar and butter in the Bowl. Pulse until fine crumbs form. Press into a springform pan and refrigerate.

Meanwhile, mix together the remaining ingredients in the Bowl until smooth. Pour into the crust and chill for at least 1 hour before serving.

CALORIES 357

FAT 29G

CHOL 80MG

SODIUM 236MG

CARB 20G

FIBER 0G

PROTEIN 8G

berry berry crisp

SERVES 8 TO 10

4 cups mixed strawberries, blackberries
    and raspberries

½ cup sugar

2 tbsp. minute or instant tapioca

1 tsp. fresh lime juice

Topping:

⅓ cup walnuts, chopped

¼ cup butter, cut in small pieces

½ cup unbleached, all purpose flour

⅓ cup sugar

¼ tsp. baking powder

pinch salt

CALORIES 176

FAT 7G

CHOL 12MG

SODIUM 58MG

CARB 28G

FIBER 2G

PROTEIN 1G

Preheat the oven to 375°F and lightly coat a 9 x 9-inch baking pan with cooking spray. Set aside.

Place the mixed berries in a bowl and add the sugar, tapioca and lime juice. Toss to coat evenly. Spoon into the prepared pan.

Place the walnuts, butter, flour, sugar, baking powder and salt in the Bowl. Pulse until the walnuts are chopped and the mixture is crumbly. Scatter the topping over the fruit and bake for 35 to 40 minutes until bubbly.

Soups, Sides, Entrées and More!

mango peach frozen yogurt

SERVES 4

½ cup frozen mango chunks

½ cup frozen peaches

2 cups low fat vanilla yogurt

Place the mango, peaches and yogurt in the Bowl. Pulse until smooth. Serve right away.

CALORIES 102

FAT 2G

CHOL 2MG

SODIUM 85MG

CARB 5G

FIBER 1G

PROTEIN 12G

dark chocolate & cherry cookies

MAKES 3 DOZEN

½ cup butter

3 egg whites

1 tsp. vanilla extract

1 cup dark brown sugar

1 tsp. ground cinnamon

1 cup whole wheat pastry flour

1 cup oat bran

1 tsp. baking soda

¼ tsp. salt

1 tbsp. ground flaxseeds

1 cup dark semi-sweet chocolate chips

1 cup dried sweet cherries, roughly chopped
(or use dried cranberries)

Preheat oven to 350°F. Place the Dough Blade in the Bowl and add the butter, egg whites and vanilla. Pulse until creamy. Add the sugar, cinnamon, flour, oat bran, baking soda, salt, and flaxseeds and pulse until just combined. Transfer to a mixing bowl and add the chocolate chips and cherries by hand. Cover and chill for 10 minutes.

Drop the dough by tablespoons onto nonstick cookie sheets, leaving an inch between each cookie. Bake until golden, about 10 minutes.

CALORIES 200

FAT 6G

CHOL 7MG

SODIUM 137MG

CARB 38G

FIBER 3G

PROTEIN 4G

48

Soups, Sides, Entrées and More!

fruit crostada

SERVES 6 TO 8

¼ cup sugar

2 cups flour

½ tsp. kosher salt

1 cup cold butter, cut into small pieces

¼ cup ice water

2 cups fresh fruit, roughly cut

3 tbsp. superfine sugar

Position the Dough Blade in the Bowl and add the sugar. Pulse for 30 seconds. Add the flour and salt and pulse again. Add the butter and pulse until the mixture resembles small peas.

Pour the ice water through the pour-spout and pulse quickly, just until the dough starts to form a mixture.

Spoon out onto foil and quickly press together to form a rough disk. Cover and chill for 1 hour or in the freezer for 15-20 minutes.

Preheat the oven to 450°F. Heavily flour a large piece of plastic wrap and quickly add the dough. Cover with another floured piece of wrap and roll to an 11-inch circle. Remove the wrap pieces and place the dough on a cookie sheet. Toss the fruit gently with sugar and place in the center of the dough, leaving a 1½-inch border. Fold up and pleat around the outside edge to encase the fruit. Bake for 20-25 minutes, or until the dough is golden.

CALORIES 380

FAT 24G

CHOL 61MG

SODIUM 310MG

CARB 40G

FIBER 1G

PROTEIN 4G

queensland banana bread

MAKES 1 LOAF; 10 SERVINGS

¼ cup butter

1 egg

¾ cup sugar

2 bananas, peeled and cut in half

3 tbsp. whole milk

½ tsp. baking soda

½ tsp. baking powder

2 cups unbleached, all-purpose flour

½ cup macadamia nuts, chopped

Preheat the oven to 350°F. Position the Dough Blade into the Bowl. Add the butter, egg, sugar, bananas and milk to the Bowl and pulse until combined. Add the soda, powder, flour and macadamias and pulse again briefly. Scrape down the sides of the Bowl as needed.

Lightly coat a 9 x 5-inch loaf pan with cooking spray and spoon the bread into the pan. Bake for 30 to 40 minutes, or until a toothpick comes out clean in the middle. Cool before slicing.

Soups, Sides, Entrées and More!

sweet carrot cookies

MAKES ABOUT 3 DOZEN COOKIES; 2 COOKIES PER SERVING

1 cup vegetable shortening

¾ cup sugar

2 eggs

1 cup carrots, peeled, grated

2 cups flour

2 tsp. baking powder

½ tsp. salt

Preheat the oven to 375°F.

Position the Dough Blade in the Bowl and add all ingredients. Pulse just until combined. Do not over-mix. Drop the batter by teaspoons onto a cookie sheet that has been lightly coated with cooking spray. Bake for 8 to 10 minutes.

CALORIES 196

FAT 12G

CHOL 27MG

SODIUM 118MG

CARB 20G

FIBER 1G

PROTEIN 7G

Soups, Sides, Entrées and More!